SNOW DAY

by BETSY MAESTRO • Illustrated by GIULIO MAESTRO

SCHOLASTIC INC.
New York Toronto London Auckland Sydney

The artist wishes to thank the Oshkosh Truck Corporation,
whose photographs of snow removal equipment were used as
reference for the illustrations in this book.

ISBN 0-590-41284-1

Text copyright © 1989 by Betsy Maestro.

Illustrations copyright © 1989 by Giulio Maestro.

12 11 10 9 8 7 6 5 4 3 2   1 2 3 4 5 6/9

Printed in the U.S.A.   08

Weather watchers had been predicting a big snowstorm for days. In the afternoon, the skies grew gray and cloudy. The smell of snow was in the air. Then, during the night, the storm moved in, blanketing the town with heavy layers of snow.

Even before the snow stopped falling, town work crews were out with their trucks to begin the long, hard job of digging out. No one else ventured into the deep snow.

In the morning, everything is white and still. The storm is over, but the town seems buried in deep drifts that cover the roads and sidewalks.

All over town, as families wake up, radios are turned on.
"No school today," they hear. School buses can't move
through the snow. It is a SNOW DAY!

For the children, it's a holiday! They go sledding and build snow people. Soon, snowballs are flying in all directions!

But for most grown-ups, the snow is a big problem.
No one can get to work. Stores, offices, schools, highways,
and airports are closed until the roads can be cleared.
Everything has come to a standstill.

Up and down the streets, people come out to shovel and sand their sidewalks and driveways. Neighbors help each other out, using snowblowers to get the job done.

Workers arrive to make repairs and to clear away the trees
and branches that fell on telephone and electric lines.

The work crews that have been out all night are still busy clearing the streets in town. Their trucks have heavy chains on the tires to keep them from getting stuck.

The plows push the snow to the side of the road as they go. Sand is dumped out on the roads to make them less slippery.

Most highways were closed during the storm, but a few cars became stranded, trapped in the heavy snow. The State Police helped the passengers to safety.

Now, tow trucks move the cars out of the way. The Highway Department has hundreds of big trucks at work, plowing and sanding the highways that crisscross the state.

At the airport, planes could not take off or land during the storm. The runways were snow-covered and pilots could not see well. Incoming planes could not land and were sent to other airports. In the morning, giant plows and snowblowers clear the runways.

Sweepers remove the remaining snow. Tank trucks spray a special liquid on the runways to melt the ice. Soon, the airport will be back in operation.

As the snow piled up, the trains also stopped running. They'll start moving again as soon as the tracks are clear. V-shaped plows, mounted on the front of engines, push the snow off the tracks.

Crews clear the rest of the snow with shovels. Heaters in the tracks may be used to melt the snow and ice. In other places, fires are started instead.

A big snowfall also causes trouble in the ports and harbors. Boats and ships cannot move freely on the rivers or into seaports if snow and ice are blocking the way.

Strong ships called "icebreakers" are sometimes needed to help keep the waterways open.

In the nearby city, the job of clearing heavy snow is really a tough one. City workers must put in many extra hours. Garbage trucks with plows push the snow into huge piles against the curbs.

The snow is trucked away so that cars can park.
There are so many sidewalks and streets to clear and sand.
A busy city cannot stay shut down for long.

Back in town, the last of the smaller roads have been cleared. Sidewalks and parking lots have all been shoveled.

The roads are sanded one more time before the trucks
head back to the garage.

At day's end, the children have tired of playing in the snow
and the work crews are glad the job is done. They can go
home to a much-needed rest.

Everything has returned to normal. Cars are out and moving again. Stores are open and the school buses are ready to roll in the morning.

But winter has just begun. Other storms will bring more snow to be cleared. But for now, this SNOW DAY is over.